TENNIS

Christine Truman

Silver Burdett Press
Morristown, New Jersey

WORLD OF SPORT

Cover: Chris Evert-Lloyd, one of the top players in the world.

Fishing
Gymnastics
Judo
Soccer
Swimming and diving
Tennis

Editor: Nick Wallwork
Editor, U.S. Edition: Joanne Fink
Researchers: Katherine Jarman/ Craigie Robertson Limited

First published in 1987 by
Wayland (Publishers) Ltd
16 Western Road, Hove
East Sussex, BN3 1JD, England

© Copyright 1987
Wayland (Publishers) Ltd

© 1987 – this adaptation,
Silver Burdett Press,
Published in the United States
by Silver Burdett Press,
Morristown, New Jersey

Designed and typeset by
DP Press Ltd, Sevenoaks, Kent

Printed in Italy
by Sagdos

Library of Congress Cataloging-in-Publication Data

Truman, Christine.
   Tennis.

   (The World of sport)
   Bibliography: p.
   Includes index.
   Summary: Examines the history, equipment, tactics, remarkable feats and players, tournaments, recent developments, and other aspects of tennis.
   1. Tennis—Juvenile literature.   2. Tennis.
I. Title.   II. Series: World of sport (Morristown, N.J.)
GV995.T75   1987   796.342′2   87–12946
ISBN 0–382–09489–1 (lib. bdg.)
ISBN 0–382–09494–8 (pbk.)

The author and publishers would like to thank Max Robertson, BBC commentator at Wimbledon for forty years, for his help and advice in the preparation of this book.

Picture acknowledgements
The pictures in this book were supplied by the following: Advantage International 14, 15, 16; All-Sport 37, 53; Mary Evans Picture Library 5, 6, 7, 8; Michael Cole Camerawork 19, 20, 24, 27, 29, 30, 31, 34; Sporting Pictures (UK) Ltd 4, 9, 10, 11, 12, 13, 17, 18, 21, 22, 23, 25, 26, 32, 33, 35, 36, 40, 41, 43, 45, 48, 49, 51, 52, 55, 56, 59, 60. All artwork by Carolyn Scrace.

Contents

History of the game	4
Recent developments	9
The life of a professional player	13
Varieties of the sport	17
Players and teams around the world	20
Stadiums	26
Championships and tournaments	30
Clothes and equipment	33
Fitness and training	38
Skills and tactics	41
Remarkable feats	61
Glossary	62
Books to read	63
Useful addresses	63
Index	64

History of the game

How many people realize that the game we call tennis is in fact only just over one-hundred years old? Lawn tennis, to give the sport its correct title, is descended from a much older game known as court tennis in the United States and real tennis in Britain. Although this kind of tennis dates back to medieval times, it is still played today on special courts in Britain, France, and the United States.

Even before the invention of court or real tennis, games involving a ball and stick had been common. An illustration on the tomb of King Beni Hassan shows ancient Egyptian women playing an early form of tennis. The ancient Greeks and Romans also played similar games to improve their fitness and strength.

Tennis, as we know it today, is based on a game called court tennis. This tennis court at Hampton Court Palace was originally built by Henry VIII in 1508.

Court tennis

Court tennis itself almost certainly originated in medieval France, where it was first played by monks. The new game soon became popular with French royalty and by 1598 there were 250 courts in Paris alone. It was not long before court tennis reached Britain and found favor with the monarchy. The tennis court built by Henry VIII at Hampton Court Palace is now the oldest in existence.

The game was similar to modern lawn tennis, but was played on a stone court using an extremely hard ball. Not surprisingly, all attempts to transfer court tennis to grass courts were unsuccessful, because the ball refused to bounce.

This problem was solved in 1850 by the invention of the rubber ball. The mechanical lawnmower, too, was invented in this period, and welcomed by groundskeepers all over the world as lawns had previously been cut with scythes.

This picture shows a game of *sphairistike*, or "sticky" in progress.

The earliest version of modern lawn tennis was "Field Tennis," invented around 1767. For a time this game was so popular that in England it threatened to overthrow the national sport of cricket. However, its popularity was short-lived, and court tennis enjoyed a revival in Victorian times.

"Sticky"

Far more important, in terms of its influence upon the modern game, was *sphairistike* (Greek for "a ball game"), which was found so difficult to pronounce that it was usually shortened to "sticky". The game was invented in 1874 by Major Walter Wingfield, who patented his invention and sold it in boxed sets, each containing a net and posts, balls, four rackets, and a book of rules similar to those used today.

"Sticky" was an instant success, partly because both men and women could play the new game (the strength required to make the ball bounce on the stone court had prevented most women from playing court tennis) and partly because it was played outdoors.

Major Walter Wingfield invented the game of "sticky" in 1873.

(Opposite, bottom) Tennis was first played at Wimbledon in 1877. This picture shows a game between Lawford and Renshaw in 1881.

Tennis soon became popular throughout the world. This Davis Cup match between England and Italy took place in 1926.

Lawn tennis was now no longer just a game, but had become a competitive sport. In 1877 the first Wimbledon championships took place. Unlike today's tournament only men's singles were played. Women were not allowed to play at Wimbledon until 1884.

The modern game

Four factors laid the foundations that changed lawn tennis from these basic beginnings into the multi-million dollar sport it is today. First, its popularity quickly spread from Britain to other parts of the world. Mary Ewing Outerbridge introduced the game to the United States in 1874. While vacationing in Bermuda she saw some British men playing the game, purchased equipment, and brought it home to Staten Island with her. There, she and her brother set up the first lawn tennis court in this country. The first U.S. Championship was played in Newport, Rhode Island, in 1881. In France it was first played in 1877. The first foreign competitors arrived at Wimbledon in 1884.

A second reason was that women rapidly became involved in the new sport: the first American ladies' singles championship took place in 1887; and in 1913 ladies' and mixed doubles were introduced at Wimbledon. Third, the game became organized. The United States National Lawn Tennis Association (now the United States Tennis Association – USTA) was established in 1881. The Lawn Tennis Association (LTA) of Great Britain dates from 1888. By 1913 the sport was so widespread that the International Lawn Tennis Federation (ILTF), the governing body of tennis, was founded in Paris.

Finally, the popularity of lawn tennis was greatly helped by the development of the media, particularly television. The first radio broadcast from Wimbledon took place in 1927, and ten years later the championships were the subject of the first ever out-of-doors broadcast by BBC television (although the first color transmission was not until 1967). Today, coverage of the Wimbledon men's singles final is sold to more than eighty television networks worldwide. This represents a much larger audience than the crowd of two hundred who paid just one shilling each to watch the first final in 1877!

Despite their unsuitable dress, women played competitively at Wimbledon from 1884 on.

Recent developments

The most important development in the last thirty years of tennis has been the rise of professionalism and the consequent introduction of "open" tournaments (that is, those open to both amateurs and professionals). In the early days of tennis, it would have been unthinkable for a player to make money from the game: a sport was traditionally played for the love of it. However, as the standard of the game rose, and the top players began to look upon tennis as a full-time occupation, it became obvious that they would soon come to depend upon it for their livelihood. In the early 1960s, more and more players began to turn professional against the wishes of the ILTF. The argument peaked in 1967 when Great Britain announced that it would hold "open" tournaments the following year.

The first tournament for professional players took place at Bournemouth, England in 1968.

Despite widespread opposition from other countries, the first open competition, the British Hard Court Championships, took place at Bournemouth in April 1968, and was won by Australia's Ken Rosewall. Amateurs and professionals played alongside each other for several years, but today all top players are professionals, and the various international team tournaments such as the Davis Cup are no longer restricted to amateurs.

Hand-in-hand with the rise of professionalism came a growing awareness among players of the need to form an organization that would protect their professional interests. Thus the chief "union" for male players, the Association of Tennis Professionals (ATP) was formed in 1972 by over sixty top players.

The ATP first demonstrated its power in 1973, when it ordered its members to withdraw from that summer's Wimbledon because of an argument with the Yugoslavian LTA. In all, seventy-three members boycotted the 1973 championships, which as a result were unexpectedly won by Jan Kodes of Czechoslovakia. The ATP then went on to lift the restriction on professionals taking part in the Davis Cup.

Jan Kodes was the surprise winner of Wimbledon in 1973 after many players boycotted the event on the orders of the ATP.

The organization for top women players is called the Women's Tennis Association (WTA), formed a year after the ATP in 1973. The WTA has campaigned strongly for equal amounts of prize money to be awarded to male and female players, on the grounds that both provide equal entertainment: in pre-WTA days it was not unusual for tournament promoters to offer $50,000 in men's prize money and only $7,000 for women.

Money has poured into professional tennis with sponsors competing fiercely for the top names.

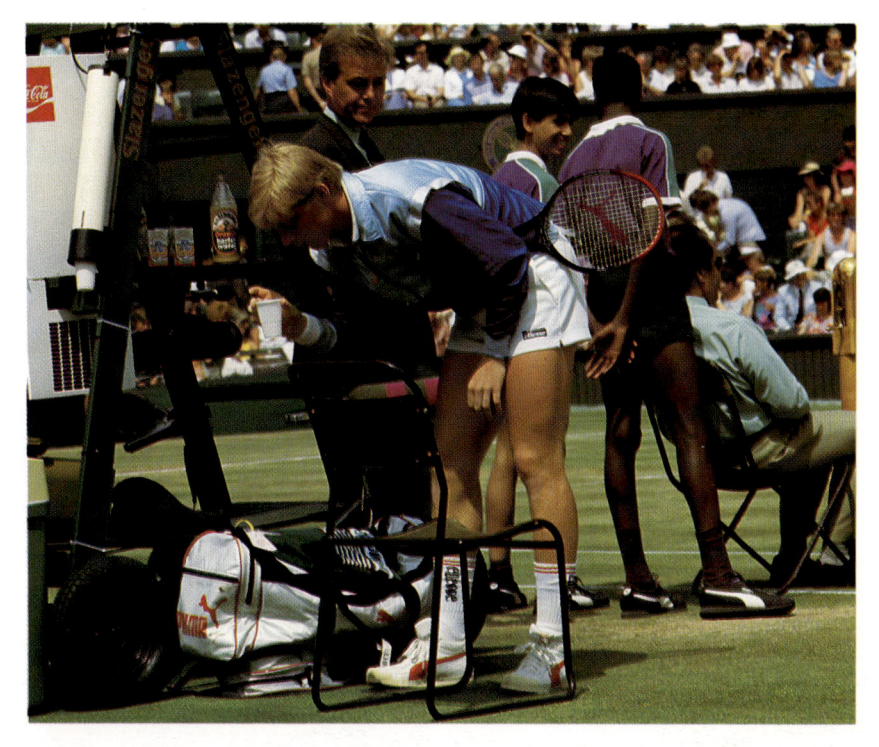

    The ATP and WTA feed members' results into a computer, which produces the world rankings. It is from these lists that the seedings for tournaments are calculated. This system, however, leads to problems with the seeding of grass court competitions because the majority of results fed into the computer are achieved on clay, cement, or carpet surfaces. So a player could be ranked number one in the world without having won a match on grass. Because Wimbledon is now the world's last major grass court championship, the seedings adapted annually from the ATP and WTA rankings invariably prove unreliable: in 1985, for example, only five of the sixteen men's seeds at Wimbledon did as well as expected. Short of creating two separate groups of rankings, it is difficult to see how this problem can be solved.

    Another feature of modern tennis, as of all sports today, is the extensive sponsorship of tournaments and even players by commercial organizations. Many companies now realize that having their names associated with top sporting events helps their reputation, and increases public awareness of their products. In 1986 the Grand Prix Series of competitions was sponsored by Nabisco cereals, while the women's tour has been known since it started as the Virginia Slims Circuit.

(Above and right) Scoreboards have come a long way since the large bead boards used at the early tournaments.

The "magic eye" is now used in tournaments throughout the world, to judge whether the ball is in or out.

A second way in which a company can get its name noticed is through sponsorship of actual players. For example, a large firm manufacturing tennis clothing will agree to pay a player if he or she will wear their clothes.

One final way in which tennis has changed considerably from its early stages is in the field of scientific achievement. We have already looked at the use of computers to produce world rankings of top players, but this is not the only contribution made by technology. Methods of scoring, too, have become more sophisticated, and the old hand-operated scoreboards have all been replaced by electronic versions. Umpires can now judge whether a service is in or out by using a machine called the "magic eye". This is an electronic device which records which side of the service line a ball has landed.

Advances in materials have also brought about changes in players' equipment. Graphite rackets are now a common sight, not only at major tournaments but also in local clubs and parks. Tennis rackets were, until the 1960s, traditionally wood-framed, but today metal, fiberglass, and graphite are all common materials.

The life of a professional player

Top competitive tennis was, until twenty years ago, simply a matter of playing and practicing. There were no sponsorship contracts, nor did players have to worry about details such as hotel accommodations for tournaments abroad, since these were always arranged by the host country.

Today, of course, there are much greater demands on a player's time. Sponsorship deals are now part of players' lives at tournaments all over the world, and a player may be paid to use or wear manufacturers' equipment. Modern tennis has also seen the rise of management agencies, which have taken over the day-to-day running of players' lives.

One such agency is Advantage International. They represent many of the world's top players, including the top British player, 26-year-old Jo Durie. Jo's lifestyle is typical of professional tennis players all over the world so let's take a look at the days leading up to her appearance in the 1986 French Open.

Saturday, April 26: Jo and her coach Alan Jones have decided that the best preparation for the French championships will be the German Open in Berlin, as both are played on slow clay surfaces. But before she can begin practicing for the Berlin tournament, Jo first has to host a "tennis clinic" for children which has been organized by her sponsors, Pilkington Glass. At these tennis clinics Jo and her coaches teach youngsters all about the skills of tennis and offer them advice on their games.

Monday, April 28: Today Jo learns that her computer ranking has gone up to number twenty-four. This position is not the highest she has ever achieved – in January 1984 Jo was the world's number five – but it is an improvement on recent rankings. The computer rankings change every two weeks to keep pace with the constant flow of Grand Prix and Virginia Slims results, and form the basis of the seedings at top tournaments.

Wednesday, May 7: Jo calls Advantage International to ask them to book her hotel for the French Open: she usually telephones the agency before trips abroad to check that her accommodations and equipment are in order. Jo's playing wear is provided by Reebok, the tennis clothing

Jo Durie has been one of Britain's top players for many years.

Coaching clinics like this are held all over the tennis playing world.

manufacturers, while her rackets are supplied by Fischer of Austria. She usually takes about twelve rackets with her to tournaments, and at least four pairs of shoes: each pair has an average life of only two weeks! In addition, different types of shoes are needed for the different playing surfaces.

Thursday, May 8: Today Jo leaves for Berlin. The agency has helped her arrange a visa, but players usually pay for their own air travel, often traveling in the more spacious first class cabins where there is less danger of their muscles stiffening up.

Friday, May 9: Jo usually finds it best to rest and relax the day after traveling, so today she only has a short practice session lasting about two hours.

Saturday, May 10 and Sunday, May 11: The real preparation for the coming matches takes place over the weekend. A typical practice session for Jo begins with ten or twenty minutes of stretching to prepare her body for the work ahead: after serious back problems nearly ended her playing career a few years ago, Jo now ensures that she is thoroughly warmed-up before hitting a single ball. The stretching exercises are followed by some gentle shots to sharpen her concentration. Then the main part of the session begins: Alan Jones makes Jo work very hard indeed, particularly at moving quickly about the court, which tends to be a problem because of her height (at 5ft. 10in. Jo is one of the tallest women players on the circuit).

Monday, May 12: Today the tournament begins, with Jo seeded number nine. Jo beats her first-round opponent, Argentina's Emilise Raponi Longo, in straight sets (7–6, 6–3): a good win, although the tie-breaker in the first set produces some anxious moments before being won 11–9 by Jo.

Tuesday and Wednesday, May 13–14: Jo defeats Iva Budarova of Czechoslovakia then Catarina Lindquist of Sweden. These victories take her through to the quarter-final of the competition.

Thursday, May 15: The player Jo must now face is the world's number one, the seemingly invincible Martina Navratilova. Jo did manage to take Navratilova to three close sets in the final of the 1984 Australian Open so she does have a chance. Unfortunately, this time Jo is beaten 2–6, 1–6, and so is out of the competition.

Jo and her coach Alan Jones advise and encourage young players to work hard at their game.

Professional tennis places great demands on a player – but the rewards can be substantial.

Saturday, May 17: All is not lost for Jo, however, for she has meanwhile managed to reach the semi-finals of the doubles with her British partner Anne Hobbs. By coincidence the players who knock them out are Martina Navratilova and her partner, Hungary's Andrea Temesvari. Jo receives $3,000 prize money for reaching the quarter-finals, and she and her partner share $2,400 for their performance in the doubles competion.

Sunday, May 18: Jo now returns to England for some more clay court practice, preparing to leave again for Paris at the end of the month.

Varieties of the sport

Different surfaces

The move to artificial surfaces began at the end of the last century, when tennis spread to countries other than Britain. Many soon found that grass courts did not suit their hot climate, and by 1900 a variety of hard surfaces were in use. In fact the first world clay court championships were held as early as 1914 at the Stade Français in Paris.

Today's French Open is still the world's unofficial clay court championship. It is included as one of the four Grand Slam tournaments because of its difficult slow surface.

Many hot countries switched to clay courts at the beginning of this century because of the problems they encountered maintaining grass courts.

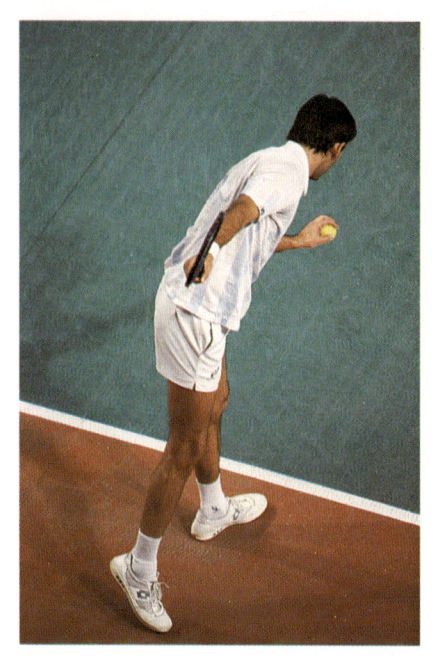

(Above) Rubberized carpet, such as this one, is a popular indoor surface.

True clay, which produces a high bounce and therefore a slow game, favors defensive players like Chris Lloyd or Ivan Lendl. More aggressive players such as John McEnroe or Martina Navratilova, will perform better on grass (which gives a low bounce and therefore a fast game) and the faster hard surfaces described below. Today there are fewer tournaments played on clay, and the clay court season now only lasts from mid-April to early June.

A top player may encounter other artificial surfaces such as rubberized asphalt which is used in the U.S. Open; cement (on which nearly all other major American tournaments are played), and indoor carpet. Amateur players will come across courts laid with red shale – Britain's equivalent of clay; or tarmac – the surface of most public parks.

The large number of court surfaces means that today's players have to be able to change their style of play to suit the court. They will also have to make changes in their equipment: for instance, Jo Durie, the player profiled in chapter three, would have changed her shoes and tightened

The Albert Hall in London provides a spectacular setting for indoor tennis.

18

the strings on her racket before setting foot on the slow-playing courts of the French Open.

Indoor tennis

Although played on different surfaces, all the tournaments mentioned above still take place outdoors. Indoor tennis, however, is becoming increasingly popular around the world. There are now, for example, both men's and women's U.S. indoor championships, while the Australian Indoors takes place in Sydney, and Stockholm is the scene of the Swedish Indoor Championships. There are many different surfaces used in indoor tennis, but the most popular at present are made of rubber, plastic, or carpet. These have only recently replaced the wooden courts that first appeared in the 1930s.

Short tennis

The newest variety of the game is called short tennis. Its aim is to get children used to the basic conditions of tennis. The game is played on a badminton court with plastic rackets and yellow foam balls. By playing short tennis a young player can begin to develop his or her concentration and acquire an eye for the ball, as well as get used to moving around the court. It is hoped that future champions will be attracted to the game at an early age through short tennis.

Many young players are being introduced to the game through short tennis.

Players and teams around the world

Because modern lawn tennis was invented in Victorian England, the early champions were all British. But it was not long before players from other countries began to overtake the game's inventors. In fact the last time the holders of both Wimbledon singles titles were British was 1934! (Fred Perry won the men's and Dorothy Round the women's.)

"The Four Musketeers"

Right from the start, countries rather than individuals seem to have dominated the game at different periods. For example, a group of Frenchmen known as "The Four Musketeers" (René Lacoste, "Toto" Brugnon, Jean Borotra,

(Below left) René Lacoste (left) and Jean Borotra, two of the "four musketeers," before a doubles match.

(Below) Suzanne Lenglen dominated the women's game in the 1920s.

(Above) For many years the Australian John Newcombe entertained crowds with his marvelous tennis and great sense of humor.

(Above right) Bjorn Borg's aggressive style of play was characterized by his powerful, double-handed backhand.

and Henri Cochet) held the men's singles title at Wimbledon from 1924 to 1929 – but what is even more remarkable is that in five out of these six matches, the losing finalist was also a Frenchman. Suzanne Lenglen, the legendary French champion, also achieved her greatest Wimbledon triumphs in this period. Similarly, the Americans dominated in the post-war years, with players like Jack Kramer and Gussy Moran (known as "Gorgeous Gussy" because of her habit of wearing lace panties under a short skirt!).

From the mid-1950s to the early 1960s it was the turn of the Australians: the great players Frank Sedgman, Lew Hoad, Ken Rosewall, Neale Fraser, John Newcombe, and Rod Laver all won major tournaments in this period.

More recently it has been the turn of the Swedish and German players following Bjorn Borg's string of wins in the 1970s and Boris Becker's Wimbledon victories.

(Above) John McEnroe's excellence has often been overshadowed by his fits of temper.

(Above center) Ivan Lendl's great strength and consistency have made him one of the world's great players.

(Above right) In 1985 Boris Becker became the youngest Wimbledon men's singles champion.

Men

IVAN LENDL (Czechoslovakia) was the world's top junior in 1978, and the world's number one in 1985. He achieved his best Wimbledon placing to date in 1986, when he was runner-up to Boris Becker. Lendl is noted for his crushing forehand and his serious approach to the game.

JOHN McENROE (USA) is one of the most brilliant player of modern times, but his all too frequent outbursts of temper have earned him the nickname "Superbrat".

McEnroe first made the headlines in 1977, when he reached the Wimbledon semi-finals as an 18-year-old qualifier. Since that date he has enjoyed great success at Wimbledon and at Flushing Meadow. McEnroe is one of several left-handed players to have made it to the top.

BORIS BECKER (West Germany) won his first Wimbledon title in 1985, breaking two records in the process: as well as becoming Wimbledon's youngest men's champion (at 17 years and 277 days) ever, he was also the first unseeded player to take the title. Becker's success seems to come from his youthful approach, and his greatest strength is his ability to raise his game on crucial points. Only time will tell if he can continue winning in the future.

Women

MARTINA NAVRATILOVA (USA) was a Czech player who defected to the United States in 1975. She uses her great physical strength to good effect in her aggressive style of play. Unlike her great rival Chris Lloyd, Navratilova is also an avid doubles player, in partnership with another top U.S. player, Pam Shriver.

CHRIS LLOYD (USA) has won every major title in tennis, including a total of eighteen "Grand Slam" competitions. When she first appeared on the circuit, Miss Evert, as she then was, was christened the "Ice Maiden" because of her expressionless face and remarkably consistent baseline game. In 1979 she married the British player John Lloyd.

HANA MANDLIKOVA (Czechoslovakia) was the Women's Tennis Association's "most impressive player" in 1979, and the circuit's "most improved player" in 1980. She has since been overshadowed by Navratilova and Lloyd, but her success in the 1985 U.S. Open proves that, on her day, she can match the best in the world.

(Above left) Martina Navratilova has dominated the women's game in recent years, using her formidable strength to great effect.

(Above center) Chris Lloyd's superb use of the double-handed backhand has encouraged many other players to adopt the stroke.

(Above right) Many people believe Hana Mandlikova to be the brightest women's prospect of the future.

The Davis Cup

As well as representing their countries as individuals, top players may also be chosen to play in the various international team tournaments. The most important of these is the Davis Cup, donated in 1900 by the American player Dwight F. Davis (in fact its correct title is "The International Lawn Tennis Championship"). At first the only competitors were Great Britain and the United States, but now some seventy nations take part annually. Matches in the early stages of the tournament are played in various geographical "zones", the winners of each zone final playing off against each other.

The Federation Cup

The Davis Cup, however, is only open to men, the equivalent for women being the Federation Cup, first played in 1963. All members of the ILTF can play, and each round includes two singles matches and one doubles. Since it started, the Federation Cup, like the Davis Cup, has been dominated by the Americans and Australians. Unlike the Davis Cup, whose rounds are spaced throughout the year and played at different localities, the Federation Cup is completed in one place within the space of a week.

The Italian and British teams line up before a Davis Cup tie.

The Wightman Cup

Another international tournament for top women players is the Wightman Cup, contested annually between Great Britain and the United States. The two countries take turns hosting the event, in which five singles and two doubles matches are played.

In the past there have been moves to abolish the Wightman Cup, but each time players of Great Britain and the United States have supported its continuation.

The King's Cup

The King's Cup was donated by King Gustav V of Sweden, and was meant to be the indoor equivalent of the Davis Cup for European nations, but has never proved as popular as that competition.

Olympic tennis

Lawn tennis was played as an official Olympic sport between 1896 and 1924, but was then abandoned following arguments over the definition of an amateur (all Olympic competitors must be amateur sportsmen – that is, they must not make any money from their sport). However, recent years have seen a reversal of this decision, and lawn tennis will be played again at the Olympic Games in 1988.

Stadiums

Wimbledon

Wimbledon, the home of the All England Lawn Tennis and Croquet Club, is the most famous tennis stadium in the world. Every June and July, it is the scene of the All England Championships, when 400,000 or so people pass through its gates to watch the top players competing on outdoor grass courts. Its popularity is reflected in the fact that all the world's best players return to Wimbledon year after year.

From the players' point-of-view, the attraction is partly in the superb organization of the competition. The main attraction for spectators at Wimbledon is that they can watch top class tennis extremely cheaply, and at very close range. If you do not have tickets, the best way to see Wimbledon is to line up for the returned seats of the Center and Number One court ticket-holders, which are sold from about 4:30pm onward at special booths on the grounds. Since matches often continue until eight or nine o'clock at night if the light is good enough, you will then have three or four hours of tennis ahead of you for a fraction of the normal price!

Wimbledon's center court is probably the most famous tennis stadium in the world.

Flushing Meadow

Flushing Meadow in New York is the scene of the United States Open each year. This stadium replaced the outdated Forest Hills as the top site for American tennis in 1978 when the grass courts of that arena were replaced by more modern artificial surfaces. The U.S. Open takes place at the end of August and beginning of September each year, and attracts crowds of over half-a-million. Flushing Meadow is on the flight path of New York's La Guardia airport, which makes the atmosphere both noisy and lively!

American enthusiasm and the local airport create a remarkable atmosphere at Flushing Meadow.

The Roland Garros Stadium

The French Open is held each May in Paris at the Roland Garros stadium, which is named after a famous French aviator who made the first powered flight across the Mediterranean Sea. It was built when France won the Davis Cup for the first time in 1927, and so had to host the following year's competition. No existing stadium was big enough, and so the city of Paris donated a brand new site.

The Roland Garros stadium opened in 1928, with a capacity of 8,000, although the stadium has recently benefited from a major facelift. The French Open, which is also one of the Grand Slam tournaments, is played on clay courts.

The French Open is played at the Roland Garros stadium which was specially built for the event in 1928.

The Kooyong Stadium

In 1986 the Australian Open moved to a new site in Melbourne. Before that it had been played on grass in the Kooyong Stadium, which was dug out of an old aboriginal hunting ground. Now, however, the tournament is played on synthetic grass in a new stadium, which has retained the name "Kooyong".

The Foro Italico

The Foro Italico, Rome, is the scene of the annual Italian championships, first staged in 1894. This stadium is close to the ancient coliseum, and has six clay courts arranged in pairs. The Italian Open, which is held each May shortly before the French, is not one of the Grand Slam competitions, but is part of the Grand Prix circuit.

The original Kooyong Stadium, shown here, was built on the site of an old aboriginal hunting ground.

Italian players always enjoy playing in front of the enthusiastic home crowds who regularly fill the Foro Italico.

Championships and tournaments

The Grand Slam

To win the Grand Slam used to involve winning, within a single season, Wimbledon, the U.S. Open, the French Open, and the Australian Open, although the rules have recently been altered to allow the four tournaments to be won consecutively. Only four players in tennis history pulled off the earlier feat: America's Donald Budge, who won the four tournaments in 1938; Maureen ("Little Mo") Connolly, also of the United States (1953); and the Australians Rod Laver (1962 and 1969) and Margaret Court (1970).

Margaret Court, perhaps the greatest Australian women's player, won the Grand Slam in 1970.

These players, however, all won the Grand Slam at a time when all of the tournaments except the French Open were played on grass. Today, any potential Grand Slam winner must be capable of producing winning performances on four different surfaces, for he or she will not only have to play on the grass of Wimbledon, but also rubberized asphalt (U.S.

Open), clay (French Open), and synthetic grass (Australian Open). Thus the Grand Slam, never an easy achievement, has today become much more difficult.

Donald Budge of the USA was the first man to achieve the Grand Slam.

The Grand Prix series

Apart from the four Grand Slam tournaments there are many others played all over the world each year. Today around seventy major international competitions are held annually for men, and just over half that number for women. These tournaments make up the Grand Prix and Virginia Slims series for men and women, which were introduced in 1970 and 1971 respectively.

In 1985 Anne White shocked Wimbledon by turning out to play in her white bodysuit.

Wimbledon was not amused, and the tournament referee decreed that the bodysuit must go. Miss White protested that she played best in what felt most comfortable, which happened to be her bodysuit, but eventually she agreed to change and reappeared in her usual playing attire.

Young players, too, should aim for a similar balance between comfort and smartness: don't forget that it will give your opponent an important psychological advantage if you walk onto the court wearing scruffy or unsuitable clothing. If you are a member of a local club, you should check their guidelines before playing there.

Shoes

Shoes are the most important part of any player's attire: it is vital that they fit properly, to enable the wearer to move around the court with comfort and confidence. The newer artificial surfaces make it less likely that you will fall, but a reasonably soft sole gives a better footing on court. It is important too, for shoes to provide proper support for the ankle: a trained clerk in a good sports shop should be able to tell you which shoes will do the job best.

Good shoes and socks are a vital part of a player's equipment.

Socks

Socks are almost as important as shoes, because they too can hinder footwork: in particular, if they are too thin you will probably develop blisters. (Some top players recommend wearing two pairs at once to reduce the likelihood of this happening). Natural fibers such as cotton or wool are preferable to artificial ones, as they allow the feet to "breathe." Specially designed tennis socks exist that reach only to the top of the instep, but these are not essential.

Most women players today wear a skirt rather than the traditional dress, which has been steadily losing its popularity. A divided skirt may prove more practical for girls than a conventional one. Whichever you choose, you should once again choose one made from natural materials such as cotton, if possible.

Incidentally, it is not advisable for young players or beginners to spend a fortune on outfitting themselves: it is best to avoid expensive, designer clothing and stick to the basics. However, one optional extra that beginners may find useful are terrycloth sweatbands: these are very good at preventing perspiration from running onto the grip of your racket.

Top players keep their warm-up tops on until the last minute to keep their muscles warm.

It is important not to let your muscles get cold or stiff. So, a warm-up suit top or warm sweater is essential before and after a game. If necessary, keep on all your extra layers until well into the start of a match, and only remove them when you are thoroughly warmed-up.

Equipment

The most basic item of equipment is, of course, the racket. It is important for young players to obtain a special junior version since any attempt to play with your mother's or father's will probably result in a strained wrist. It is best at this stage to choose a racket balanced toward the handle rather than toward the head: if not you may find that all your shots end up in the net!

Most of today's top players use a graphite racket – its strength and lightness make it an ideal material for the new large-headed rackets.

In recent years metal rackets have improved enormously and as a result have become more popular than wooden rackets. However, a young player should start by using a wooden racket which gives greater control because the ball stays on the strings longer. However, as your play progresses, you will probably want to change to a more powerful metal racket.

Whichever type of racket you choose, it will almost certainly come with a plastic or canvas head cover. This will protect the strings from rain and the frame from damage when the racket is not being used. If you do choose a wooden frame, you should also buy a racket-press so that it doesn't become warped.

Tennis balls

Wimbledon began using yellow balls for the first time in its history in 1986 (previously they had been white), and there is no doubt that the fluorescent type shows up better in poor light. For the beginner, however, a large supply of balls is more important than their color, for you will quickly become tired if you have only a few and are forced to keep stopping to collect them.

Finally, a large leather or plastic carry-all is very useful for transporting all this equipment, plus extra items such as a spare sweatshirt.

Fitness and training

Warm-up

As with any sport it is important to do a few gentle exercises to loosen up before a game of tennis or a training session. The following exercises should prove sufficient for most players. Remember that this is a warm-up, not a training routine. The exercises should be done smoothly and your breathing remain steady throughout.

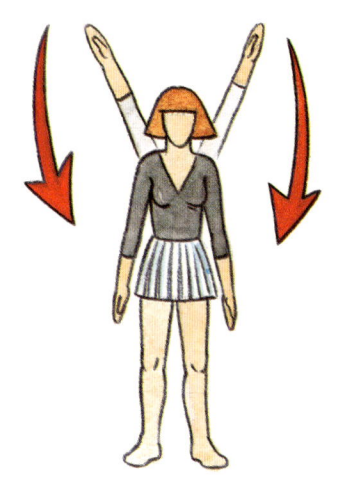

1 Shoulder rotation Feet shoulder-width apart, arms by your sides. 10 full arm circles forward, 10 backward.

2 Side bending Slide the right hand slowly down your right thigh. Push your left arm as high over your head as possible. Relax and straighten, then repeat on the left. Repeat 5 times.

3 Trunk rotation Feet apart, hands on hips. Legs straight, lean back from the waist and rotate your hips fully right and left.

4 Toe touch Feet apart, arms out to the sides. Legs straight, rotate and bend to touch left then right toes, as above, 5 times.

5 Lunge Feet well apart. Lunge right, bending your right knee and straightening your left leg. Stand, then lunge left. Repeat.

6 Ankle stretch Toes and balls of feet on a 2 inch block, arms by your sides. Slowly raise and lower heels 5 times.

Fitness

The exercises above will not only help you warm-up, but will also improve your suppleness and mobility. As well as these qualities you will also need strength, stamina, speed, and skill, to improve your game.

Strength and stamina

These two qualities must be developed if you wish to improve. It will give you a great advantage over the opposition if you are fitter than they, and will enable you to train for longer and so improve further. Some of these exercises are extensions of those done in the warm-up, but now both your breathing and heart-rate should reach a maximum.

1 Push-up Adopt the front support position, with palms under shoulders, body straight. Bend and straighten your arms without letting your legs touch the floor.

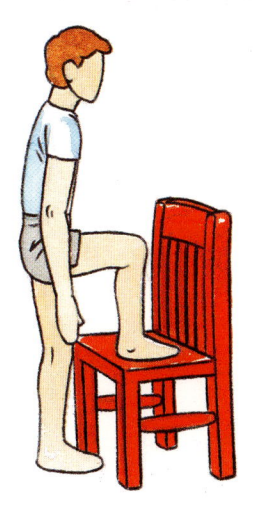

2 Step-up Step onto a bench or chair about 20 inches high and step down again with the same foot. Start half of your repetitions with the left foot and half with the right foot.

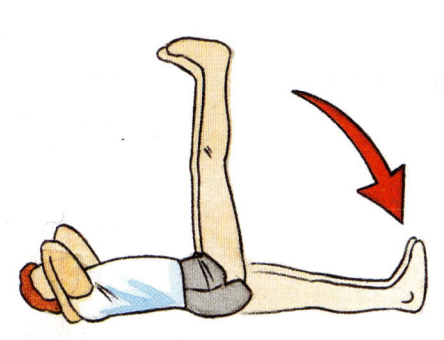

3 Leg-raise Lie flat, hands clasped behind your neck. Lock your knees and raise your legs till they are at about right angles to your body. Lower them slowly.

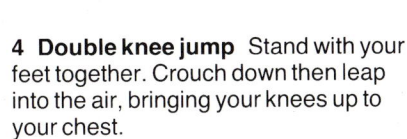

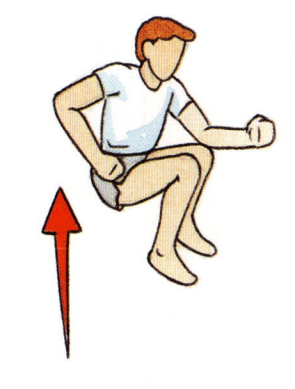

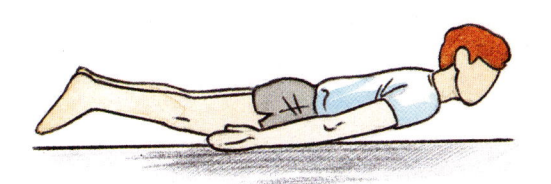

4 Double knee jump Stand with your feet together. Crouch down then leap into the air, bringing your knees up to your chest.

5 Back-arch Lie on your stomach, hands by your sides with the palms up. Slightly raise your head, chest, and legs off the floor at once.

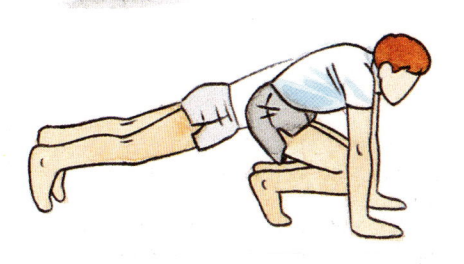

6 Squat thrust Adopt the front support position, knees between arms. Thrust backward, straightening your body and legs, and then forward again.

39

Speed

Place a number of tennis balls at various intervals between the net and the service line. Sprint from the baseline to the ball and back again. Repeat the exercise until you have collected all the balls.

Skill

The following exercise will help you change from one grip to another. At the same time you will get used to the "feel" of the ball on your racket.

Start by walking around the edge of the court bouncing the ball on the ground with your racket. When you are used to this, bounce the ball on top of the racket then against the ground. Try the exercise while jogging around the court.

These two exercises may be useful as warm-up exercises before starting a game.

(Left) Speed around the court is vital on grass courts where the ball can be hit in a way that will make it stop suddenly.

Skills and tactics

"Practice makes perfect" is a saying that is true of any sport. However, if you are really eager to play tennis, then you will probably enjoy the practice almost as much as the games themselves. One way to develop skills, and the way in which many of the top players started, is simply to find a wall and hit a ball against it for hours on end. This exercise has two advantages: it trains you first to watch the ball, and secondly to place your shots. If you want to make the procedure more difficult, try marking the wall with chalk crosses where you want the ball to hit it. Or try hitting some shots from a fair distance away (the equivalent of a baseline shot) and others from very close to the wall (as you would for a volley).

Position of readiness

The picture on the right shows the correct stance to adopt when waiting to receive a service or shot in a rally.
- Keep your knees slightly bent and your body weight on the front of your feet.
- Hold the racket well in front of the body. This will help you to open up your strokes.
- Support the racket with the left hand. This helps to keep the head of the racket up, ready for the next stroke.

If you want to improve your game it is important to receive proper coaching.

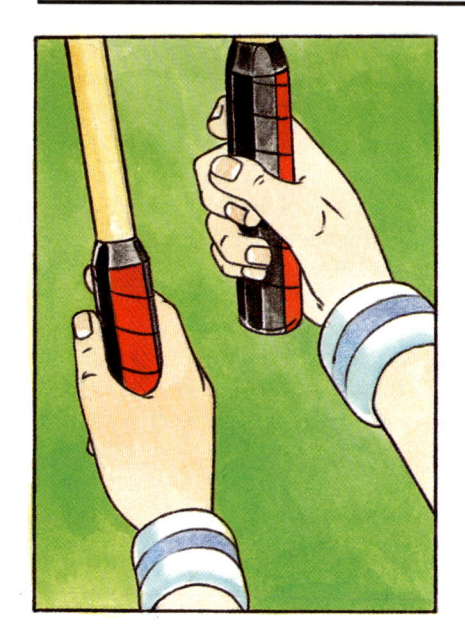

Forehand drive

Grip

The grip used for the forehand drive is often called the "shake-hands" grip because the racket is held as if you are shaking hands with it. To get this grip, hold the racket in your left hand, just below the head of the racket and turn the strings vertically to the ground. Put your right hand against the strings of the racket and slide your hand down to the grip. Now close your fingers around it.

Make sure that your fingers are not bunched up together. Spread them slightly until they feel comfortable. Your forefinger should be pushed upward as though gripping the trigger of a gun. The "V" formed between the thumb and the forefinger should fall on the same line as the red area in the diagram on the left.

1 The right foot should be placed at a right-angle to the flight of the ball. The left shoulder should be turned away from the ball and the racket brought backward.

2 The left foot should be positioned according to height and speed of the ball. Knees should be slightly bent.

3 Contact with the ball should be made just in front of the left foot. The wrist should be firm and the arm swinging freely.

Chris Lloyd shows superb balance and positioning as she prepares to play a forehand drive. Notice how her eye is on the ball and her arms spread to balance herself as she prepares to play the shot.

4 The right arm and the body follow through. The left foot remains firmly planted.

The stroke
Practice the forehand drive without a ball to get used to the swing of the racket. When you feel comfortable with the stroke, throw a ball in the air with your left hand, let it bounce once, then hit it across the net. The next stage is to get someone to either throw or hit the ball across the net to you. Concentrate on positioning the ball in different parts of the court when you return it.

Backhand drive

Most players find the backhand a more difficult shot than the forehand, but this is largely because they fail to position themselves correctly. You will never master this stroke unless you ensure that you are standing at a right angle to the net – that is, parallel to the line of the ball. Body positioning is a skill which takes some time to acquire, and it is important not to develop bad habits in the early stages which will prove difficult to shake off at a later date.

Grip

Start by holding the racket with the forehand grip. Keep the racket in the same position with your left hand, then move your hand counter-clockwise around the grip until your palm is on top of the handle. The "V" formed by your thumb and forefinger should fall on the line of the grip shown in the diagram on the left.

The stroke

1 As the ball comes toward you, place your left foot at a right angle to the ball. Adjust to a backhand grip as the racket moves backward.

2 The right foot comes across and the leading shoulder turns away from the ball.

3 Contact with the ball should be made just in front of the right foot, this enables you to lean into the shot.

4 The follow-through should be carried through to shoulder height. The body should remain sideways to the net.

(Above) Boris Becker prepares to play a backhand drive. His racket is held high and his right leg has come across his body as he prepares to drive the racket through the ball.

45

The service

The stroke

1 Stand with your left foot just behind the base line at an angle of 45°. Your feet should be a comfortable distance apart. The racket should be held at waist level, supported with your left hand, and pointing in the direction of service. The ball is held in the fingertips of the left hand against the neck of the racket.

2 As the racket moves backward you should move your straightened left arm simultaneously for the toss.

3 Your weight should be on your front foot as the ball is released. The racket continues to move backward and behind the neck.

The service is a movement – or rather a series of movements – that requires endless practice. It often helps to break it down into four stages: the first in which the ball is thrown; the second, while the ball completes its course upward, in which you reach down behind you with your racket (it helps to imagine that you are washing your back with a brush); the third stage involves bringing the racket up to meet the ball; and the final stage is actually striking the ball. Each of these movements has to be practiced separately before they are put together: even top players will spend hours, for example, on perfecting their toss. Once again, it is important when

4 The racket reaches its furthermost position behind the neck and the weight moves onto the back foot.

5 As the racket is thrown forward at the ball the right leg comes through. The arm should be fully extended as the racket hits the ball.

6 The follow-through comes across the body as the weight is thrown forward onto the front foot.

serving to stand at a right angle to the net; as you hit the ball the racket should travel diagonally across your body.

Grip

There are two types of grip that can be used for the service stroke. It is probably best to start by using the forehand grip until you have become used to the serving style. Once you are comfortable serving, then try a variation of the backhand grip. Grip the racket as you do for the backhand but make sure that the thumb is wrapped around the handle. Serve using the face of the racket which you used for the forehand.

As you swing your arm to hit the ball, your wrist should turn so that the open head of the racket is facing the serving area as it hits the ball. This grip will feel awkward at first, but is well worth adopting since it will enable you to serve harder and to impart spin and swing on the ball.

Never rush your serve. In this picture you can see Gabriela Sabatini of Argentina thinking carefully before throwing the ball into the air.

Once you have thrown the ball into the air, keep your eye on it throughout the service movement. When you first start serving, it is a good idea to practice throwing the ball at the correct height. Once this has become instinctive, you can concentrate on perfecting the rest of your service motion.

The forehand and backhand volley

Most players find the volley a considerably easier shot than the service, possibly because it is more of a "reflex action": shots come at you so quickly when you are at the net that your immediate instinct is simply to hit them! The volley is a completely different type of shot from the forehand and backhand drives: it involves more of a chopping motion than a driving action. Body positioning is not so important at the net as it is for the baseline shots.

Forehand volley

Grip
The grip for the forehand volley should be the same as for the forehand drive.

The stroke

(Right) Jo Durie leans nicely into a forehand volley. The shot appears to be coming nicely off the center of the racket, but Jo probably wishes she'd played the shot closer to the net.

1 Move into the ready position about six to seven feet from the net. The knees should be bent and the racket cradled in your free hand. The head of the racket should be held close to shoulder level.

2 As the ball approaches, turn your shoulder and move toward the ball with your left foot.

3 Contact with the ball should be made just in front of the left foot. You should keep your wrist firm and concentrate on hitting the ball with the center of the racket. There is no follow through for the forehand volley.

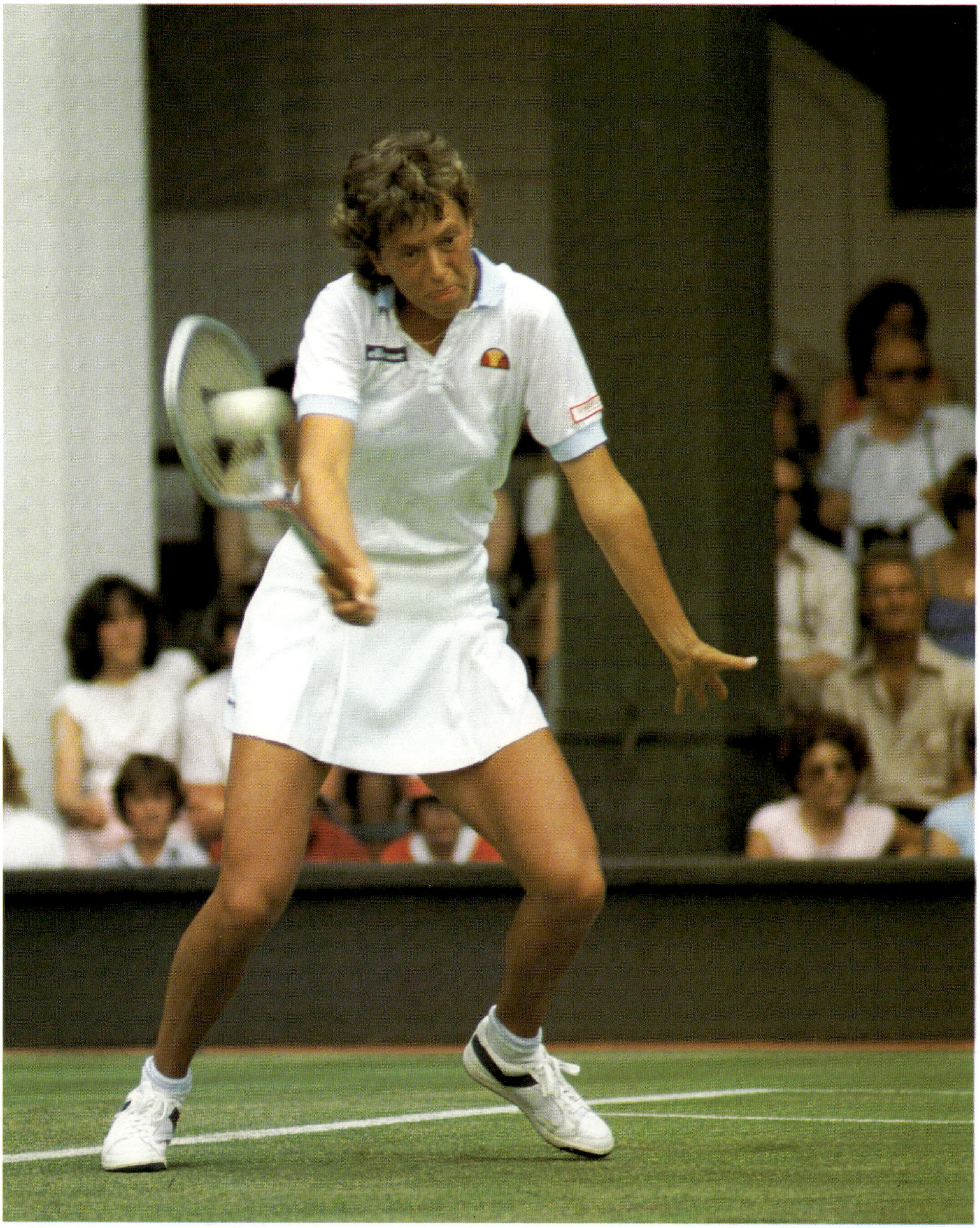

Backhand volley

Grip
The grip should be the same as for the backhand drive.

(Opposite page) This spectacular special-effects shot illustrates the explosive power of a firm volley.

1 Move into the ready position about six to seven feet from the net. The knees should be bent and the racket cradled in the left hand – this is most important for the backhand volley.

2 Turn away from the ball as it comes toward you and move toward the oncoming ball with your right foot forward.

3 Contact with the ball should be made just in front of the right foot. The racket can be stopped at this point, or if a more powerful volley is required, you can follow through until the racket reaches shoulder height.

(Right) These two pictures show Joakim Nystrom playing a crisp backhand volley. His weight is nicely placed on his front foot and the racket stopped at the point of impact in a chopping motion.

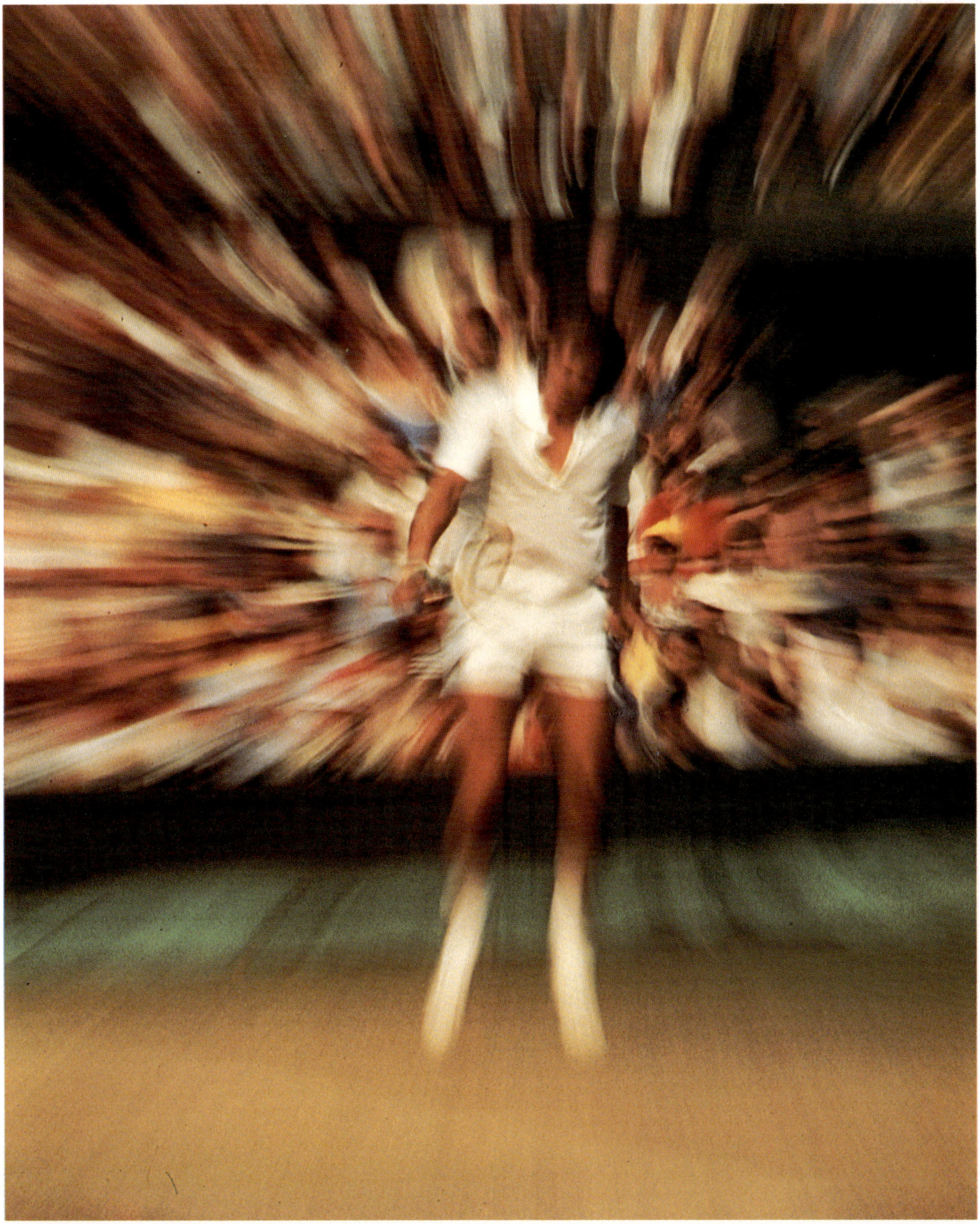

The smash

The smash is basically the service stroke without the toss. As with the service, remember to stand sideways to the line of the ball.

Grip
The grip should be the same as for the service stroke.

The stroke

1 As soon as you spot a lob you should turn sideways to the ball. Bring the racket into a semi-serving position.

2 Skip backwards, remaining sideways, to place yourself under the dropping ball. Align the ball with your left hand.

3 Stop with the weight on your back foot when you're in position. Prepare to hit the ball as you would for a serve.

4 Contact with the ball should be made at full stretch with an open racket head.

Ivan Lendl lines himself up with an overhead ball before playing a smash.

When playing a lob the ball should be pushed, rather than hit, over the head of the oncoming player.

The lob

The lob is generally used as a defensive shot to buy some time when a player is in difficulty. Although it is useful in this situation, it can be used much more effectively when your opponent is moving forward in expectation of a passing shot.

The lob shot should be "pushed" rather than hit over the net. You should try and ignore your opponent and concentrate on placing the ball as near to the baseline as you can.

The drop shot

This is the shot that falls just over the net and dies very quickly on the other side. The drop shot is very useful for breaking up an opponent's rhythm since he or she will have to scramble quickly to the net to return the ball.

It is important to disguise your drop shot or your opponent will anticipate the shot early and have no difficulty returning it. Hit slightly underneath the ball (the backspin will prevent the ball from bouncing) and try to hit the ball at the top of its bounce when it has least energy.

Checklist

- Always watch the ball right up until the moment when it is struck. Sometimes it helps to count "one-two-three" as the ball comes towards you, aiming to hit it on "three".
- Good body-positioning is vital. Remember to always stand sideways to the ball.
- Keep your racket in the "ready" position at all times when you are not actually hitting the ball.
- Concentrate throughout the game: deep breathing can sometimes help to clear your mind.

Tactics

There are two main areas of a tennis court: the backcourt and the forecourt.

The backcourt extends for a few feet inside the baseline to several yards behind the baseline. Any ball played within this area will be returned with a driving stroke. The forecourt is the area between the net and halfway to the service line. Most balls in this area should be returned with a volley.

The area between these two is a "no-mans land" which should be avoided. Move forward or backward from here depending on the strength of your shot, but never get caught standing in this area.

Movement around the court

There is a great temptation to stand still after playing a shot to see where it is going. As soon as you have played a shot, stay on your toes and move quickly to close up any space that you have left for your opponent.

There have been many studies made of the world's top tennis players. What they all show is that they win their games not through consistently playing winning shots, but by making fewer mistakes than their opponent. It is therefore vital that you play to your opponent's weaknesses and force him or her to make mistakes. At the beginning of a match start by playing a shot directly at your opponent.

No matter what the surface, all tennis courts are a standard size.

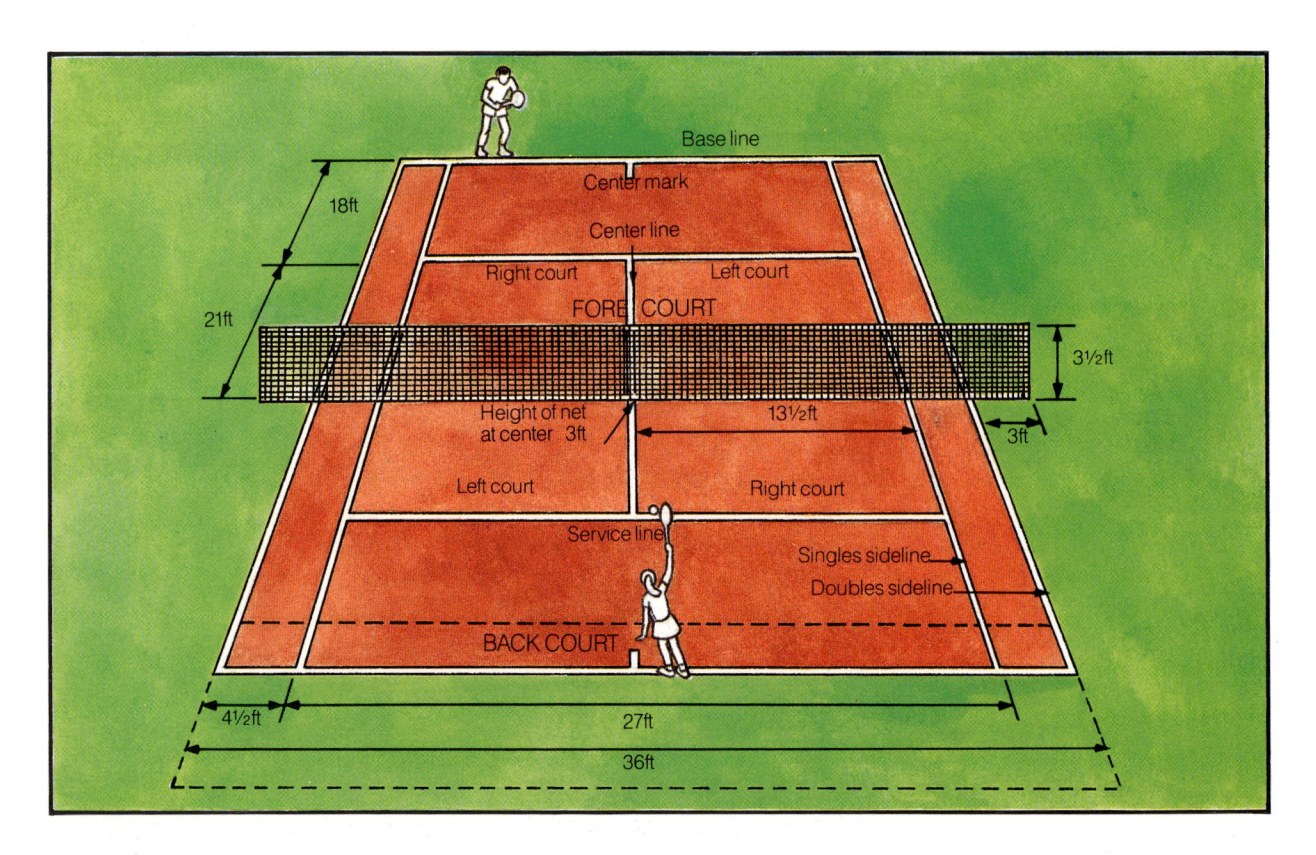

Mats Wilander rushes into position after playing a shot. Always stay on your toes and quickly consider your next option.

They will automatically move to their stronger stroke to return the ball. This will tell you which side to avoid if possible.

That does not mean however that you should play every shot to their weak side. After a while your opponent will see what your tactics are and change his or hers accordingly.

Never let your opponents get into a rhythm, always try and surprise them. If you play a hard deep shot to one side, play a looping, high-bouncing shot to the other side next time. If they are scrambling to return a shot, rush up to the net and volley their return. Before a game you could even work out a sequence of shots to play if you find yourself in a certain area of the court. In this way you can concentrate more on the shot since you don't have to worry about where to place it.

Another factor that could affect the game are the weather conditions. If the sun is in your opponent's face try and draw him or her to the net and play a lob shot. If the wind is blowing into your face then try a few drop shots just over the net, the ball will die much more quickly on a windy day.

One important point to remember, if you are well ahead using certain tactics, don't change them – never change a winning game.

With many more hours of practice, one of these children could one day become a world champion.

Remarkable feats

Fastest serve

There are many arguments about who has, or who had, the fastest serve.

In 1931, with the measuring equipment then available, William "Big Bill" Tilden was timed at 163.6 mph (263 km/h.) The fastest serve recorded on modern electronic equipment is 138 mph (222 km/h) by Steven Denton (USA) at Beaver Creek, Colorado, on July 29, 1984. However, some players and experts believe that the 1948 Wimbledon champion Bob Falkenburg (USA) was the fastest ever.

Most titles

Margaret Smith Court (AUS) won a record 63 major titles, singles and doubles, from her first Australian singles victory in 1960 to the U.S. women's doubles title. They included 10 Wimbledon wins, 18 in the U.S. championships, 22 Australian titles, and 13 French titles. She also won an additional 26 in the less important Italian, German, and South African championships, plus 4 U.S. National titles.

Battle of the sexes

Bobby Riggs (USA) the 1939 Wimbledon champion, challenged the top female players in 1963 when he was 55 years old. He first beat Margaret Smith Court (AUS) in the USA but was then soundly beaten 6–4, 6–3, 6–3, by Billie Jean King (USA) at the Houston Astrodome, in Texas. The interest aroused by the latter male vs. female game drew the largest crowd ever to watch a game of tennis – 30,472, plus an estimated television audience of 50 million.

Longest game

The longest singles game was one of 37 deuces (80 pts) between Anthony Fawcett (Rhodesia) and Keith Glass (G.B.) in the first round of the Surrey championships at Surbiton, Surrey, on May 26, 1975. It lasted 31 minutes.

Noelle Van Lottum and Sandra Begljn played a game lasting 52 minutes, in the semi-finals of the Dutch indoor championships at Ede, Gederland, on February 12, 1984.

The longest rally

The longest rally in tournament play is one of 643 times over the net between Vicky Nelson and Jean Hepner at Richmond, Virginia, in October, 1985. The 6 hour 22 minute match was won by Nelson 6–4, 7–6. It ended with a 1 hour, 47 minute tie-breaker, 13–11 for which one point took 29 minutes.

Highest earnings

Ivan Lendl (Czechoslovakia) won a men's record of $2,028,850 in 1982. The record for a woman is $2,173,556 in 1984 (including $1 million Grand Slam bonus) by Martina Navratilova.

Glossary

Baseline The line at the back of the court, running parallel to the net.
Deep shot A shot that lands near the baseline at the back of the court.
Grand Prix Series This is a league with points being won at various tournaments over the year.
Grand Slam, the To win the Grand Slam a player (male or female) must win Wimbledon, the U.S. Open, the French Open, and the Australian Open, although not necessarily in the same year.
Patent A law that prevents other people from stealing an original idea.

Qualifier A player who has to win a number of matches before being allowed to enter a tournament.
Rankings The list that gives the positions of the world's top players.
Seedings The list that shows where a player is expected to finish in a tournament.
Sponsorship Payments made to players in return for them wearing a company's clothes or using their equipment.
Straight-sets The minimum number of sets required to win a game (two for women, three for men).
Tie-breaker The scoring system used once a game has reached six or eight games all. The opponents play the best of twelve points and must win by two clear points.

Books to read

Competitive Tennis: A Guide for Parents and Young Players by David A. Benjamin (Harper and Row, 1979)
How to play Mixed Doubles by Billie Jean King, et al. (Simon & Schuster, 1980)
Official Encyclopedia of Tennis by the United States Tennis Association (Harper and Row, 1981)

Teaching Children Tennis the Vic Braden Way by Vic Braden and William Burns (Little, Brown, 1980)
Tennis my Way by Martina Navratilova and Mary Carillo (Scribners, 1983)

Useful addresses

The International Tennis Federation
Barons Court
London
W14 9EG
England

International Tennis Hall of Fame
Newport, RI

The Lawn Tennis Association
Barons Court
London
W14 9EG
England

National Tennis Foundation
100 Park Avenue
New York, NY. 10017

Tennis Australia
PO Box 343
South Yara
Victoria 3141
Australia

United States Tennis Association, Inc.
51 East 42nd Street
New York, NY 10017

Index

All England Lawn Tennis and Croquet Club 26
Association of Tennis Professionals (ATP) 10, 11
Australia 7, 9, 21, 24
Australian Open 15, 28, 30, 31

Balls 5, 37, 38, 40, 41, 43, 46, 47, 48, 54, 57, 58
Baseline 40, 41, 57, 58
Britain 4, 8, 9, 16, 17, 18, 20, 24, 25
British Hard Court Championships 9

Clothing 33–6
Courts 4, 5, 15, 35, 40, 43, 60
   backcourt 58
   cement 18
   clay 16, 17, 18, 28, 29, 31
   forecourt 58
   grass 5, 11, 17, 18, 26, 30
   indoor carpet 18
   red shale 18
   rubberized asphalt 18, 30
   stone 5, 6
   synthetic grass 28, 31
   tarmac 18
   wooden 19
Czechoslovakia 10, 15, 22, 23

Davis Cup 9, 10, 24, 25, 27
Doubles 23, 24, 25, 32

Equipment 36–7
Exercises 38–9, 40, 41

Federation Cup 24
Flushing Meadow 22, 27
Four Musketeers 20–21
France 4, 5, 7, 8, 16, 20, 21, 27, 33
French Open 13, 17, 19, 27, 28, 30, 31

German Open 13
Grand Prix series 11, 29, 31, 32
   "masters" 32
Grand Slam tournaments 17, 23, 28, 29, 30–31
Grip 40, 42, 44, 48, 51, 52, 54

International Lawn Tennis Federation (ILTF) 8, 9, 24
Italian Open 28–9

King's Cup 25

Lawn Tennis Association (LTA) 8

Practice 14, 16, 41, 43, 46

Rackets 12, 14, 19, 36, 37, 40, 41, 42, 43, 44, 46, 47, 48, 57
   graphite 12
   metal 37
   plastic 19
   wooden 37
Rankings 11, 12, 13

Shots 41, 50, 58, 59, 60
   baseline 50
   defensive 57
   drop 57, 60
Sponsorship 11, 12, 13, 14, 33
Stadiums
   Flushing Meadow 27
   Foro Italico 28
   Kooyong 28
   Roland Garros 27, 28
   Wimbledon 26
Strokes 41, 42, 43, 44, 46, 47, 48, 57, 59
   backhand drive 44, 48, 50, 52
   driving 58
   forehand drive 42, 43, 44, 48, 50, 51
   lob 57, 60
   service 41, 46, 47, 48, 50, 54
   smash 54–5

Tactics 41, 58, 59, 60
Tennis
   court 4, 5, 6
   field 6
   indoor 19
   lawn 4, 5, 7, 8, 20, 25
   real 4, 5, 6
   short 19
   sphairistike 6

Top players 12, 13, 18, 35, 41, 47
   Becker, Boris 21, 22–3
   Borg, Bjorn 21
   Durie, Jo 13, 14, 15, 16, 18
   Hobbs, Anne 16
   Kramer, Jack 21
   Lendl, Ivan 18, 22
   Lloyd, Chris 18, 23
   Mandlikova, Hana 23
   McEnroe, John 18, 22
   Moran, Gussy 21
   Navratilova, Martina 15, 16, 18, 23
   Perry, Fred 20
   Round, Dorothy 20
   White, Anne 33, 34

U.S.A. 4, 7, 8, 21, 22, 23, 24, 25, 27, 30, 32, 33
U.S. Open 18, 23, 27, 30, 31

Virginia Slims Series 11, 31, 32
Volley 41, 50, 51, 52, 58, 60
   backhand 50, 52
   forehand 50–51

Warm-up 38, 39
West Germany 22
Wightman Cup 25
Wimbledon championships 7, 8, 10, 11, 20, 21, 22, 26, 30, 33, 34, 37
Wingfield, Major Walter 6
Women's Tennis Association (WTA) 10, 11, 23